Art and Culture of the

Prehistoric World

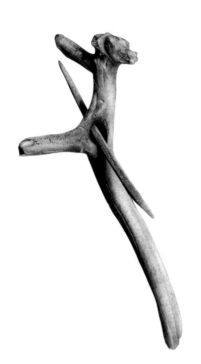

ANCIENT ART AND CULTURES

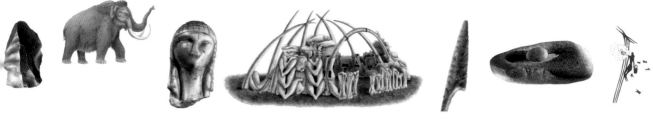

Art and Culture of the

Prehistoric World

Beatrice D. Brooke and Roberto Carvalho de Magalhães

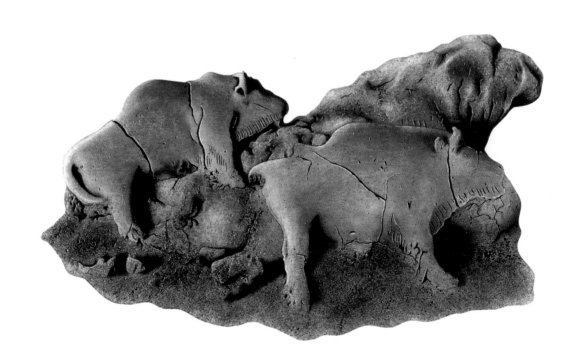

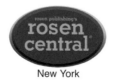
rosen
central
New York

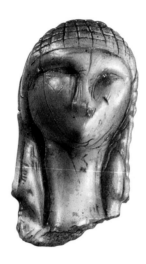

This edition published in 2010 by:

The Rosen Publishing Group, Inc.
29 East 21st Street
New York, NY 10010

Additional end matter copyright © 2010 by The Rosen Publishing Group, Inc.

Library of Congress Cataloging-in-Publication Data

Brooke, Beatrice D.
Art and culture of the prehistoric world / Beatrice D. Brooke and Roberto Carvalho de Magalhães.
  p. cm.—(Ancient art and cultures)
Includes index.
ISBN 978-1-4358-3588-7 (library binding)
ISBN 978-1-61532-879-6 (pbk)
ISBN 978-1-61532-880-2 (6 pack)
1. Prehistoric peoples. 2. Tools, Prehistoric. 3. Art, Prehistoric. 4. Antiquities, Prehistoric. I. Magalhães, Roberto Carvalho de. II. Title.
GN740.B76 2010
709.01'12—dc22

2009031774

Manufactured in the United States of America

CPSIA Compliance Information: Batch #LW10YA: For Further Information contact Rosen Publishing, New York, New York at 1-800-237-9932

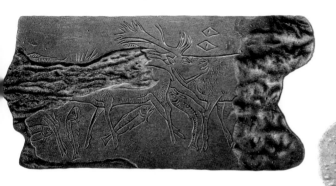

Contents

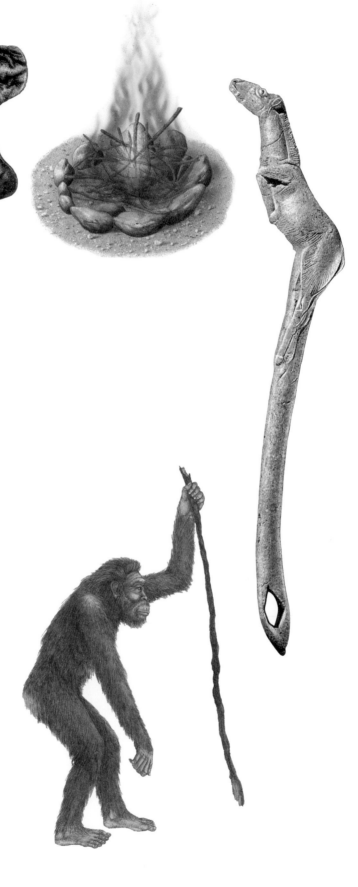

Introduction

odern humans are descended from ape-like creatures that lived in Africa several million years ago. Some time between about 6 to 4 million years ago the first species of hominid (the family to which humans belong) separated itself from other primate families, including the one that would later evolve into present-day apes, such as chimpanzees and orangutans. At about the same time our early ancestors became bipedal, which means that they stood in an upright position and walked on two legs instead of four. There followed a very long period during which evolving species of early humans with increasingly larger brains learned to make stone tools, control fire and become successful hunters. Much later, they began to use their large brains for abstract thought and it was then that they developed religion and art, among other things. Beginning about 10,000 years ago, many of them began to keep livestock and grow crops instead of hunting and gathering the food they needed. These first farmers soon grouped their makeshift houses together into more permanent villages and towns. By the 4th millennium BCE they had begun to keep written records of their doings. This long period of time up until the invention of writing is called prehistory.

Modern humans are the only surviving members of the hominid family. Hominids are part of a much larger group, or "order," called primates. The first primates appeared over 65 million years ago. The skeleton above is of a 50-million-year-old primate called Smilodectus. *It has the grasping hands, enlarged brain area and short snout typical of all primates.*

Artwork reconstruction of an Australopithecus.

Skull of Homo ergaster, *found in Kenya. It dates to between 1.7 and 1.5 million years ago. Archaeologists think that it may be an early form of* Homo erectus.

Skeleton of the Australopithecus afarensis *named Lucy (after the famous Beatles' song "Lucy in the Sky with Diamonds," a favorite with the archaeologists who discovered her in 1974).*

Dating to 3.2 million years ago, her skeleton, about 40 percent of which has been preserved, is one of the most complete specimens of an australopithecine ever found.

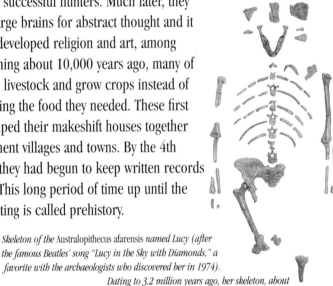

6 million years ago
5 million years ago
4 million years ago
3 million years ago
2 million years ago

1 2 3 4 5 6 7 8 9 10 11 12

Our oldest ancestors

New discoveries in the 1990s pushed the date at which hominids became separate from other primate species back even further into the past. At the moment, the oldest human fossil finds (and our oldest ancestors) are from a species named *Ardipithecus ramidus*. They date to 4.4 million years ago. Scientists are unsure of *A. ramidus*'s exact place in the human story, and are not even sure whether it walked upright.

The diagram shows the family tree of modern humans and their ancestors. It also shows the separate evolutionary branches of the modern apes. The exact relationships between the various species of hominid are not clear because archaeologists often have only incomplete skeletons from which to work.

Humans and apes

That humans and apes are closely related is shown by the fact that their skeletons match almost bone for bone. However, when our hominid ancestors began to walk upright a number of significant changes occurred.

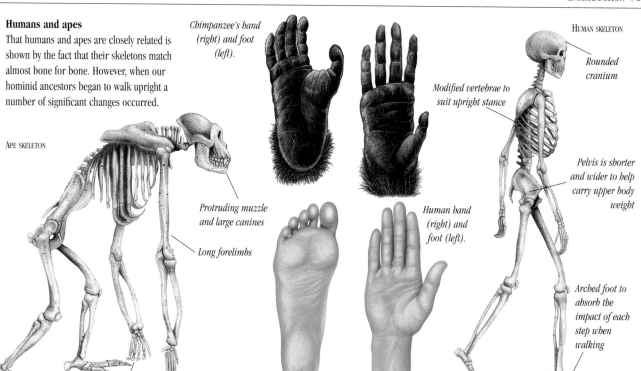

APE SKELETON

Chimpanzee's hand (right) and foot (left).

Protruding muzzle and large canines

Long forelimbs

Hands and knuckles used when walking

Modified vertebrae to suit upright stance

Human hand (right) and foot (left).

HUMAN SKELETON

Rounded cranium

Pelvis is shorter and wider to help carry upper body weight

Arched foot to absorb the impact of each step when walking

Hands and feet

Although the hands and feet of chimpanzees and humans are remarkably similar, there are some important structural differences. The flat of the chimpanzee's hand is considerably longer than its human counterpart and the fingers are more widely spaced. The chimpanzee's foot has a widely spaced "thumb." These are all adaptations for climbing and moving about in the trees. In comparison the relatively large human thumb has a much greater range of movement, making it ideal for picking up, holding onto and moving objects about. The human foot, with its arch and fleshy pads, is ideal for cushioning and balance in the upright position we use when walking.

OUR FAMILY TREE

The hominid species shown on the diagram. The dates refer to when the species lived and the place name to where its first fossils were discovered.

1. **Ardipithecus ramidus** (4.4 million years ago, Ethiopia): the oldest known hominid.
2. **Australopithecus anamensis** (4.2–3.9 million years ago, Kenya): the earliest hominid that scientists are sure walked upright.
3. **Australopithecus afarensis** (3.6–2.9 million years ago, Tanzania): the species to which the famous "Lucy" skeleton belongs.
4. **Australopithecus africanus** (3–2.3 million years ago, South Africa): the first hominid discovered in Africa in the 1920s.
5. **Australopithecus aethiopicus** (2.8–2.3 million years ago, Ethiopia).
6. **Australopithecus garhi** (2.5 million years ago, Ethiopia): may have been the first species to eat meat and use stone tools.
7. **Australopithecus boisei** (2.3–1.4 million years ago, Tanzania).
8. **Australopithecus robustus** (1.9–1.5 million years ago, South Africa): not a direct human ancestor.
9. **Homo rudolfensis** (2.4–1.8 million years ago, Kenya).
10. **Homo habilis** (1.9–1.6 million years ago, Tanzania): once thought to be the earliest tool user.
11. **Homo ergaster** (1.7–1.5 million years ago, Kenya).
12. **Homo erectus** (1.7–250,000 years ago, Indonesia): the first hominid to use fire. Emigrated from Africa and spread throughout the Old World.
13. **Homo antecessor** (800,000 years ago, Spain): the last common ancestor of Neanderthals and modern humans.
14. **Homo neanderthalensis** (200,000–30,000 years ago, Germany): mankind's last fellow species.
15. **Homo sapiens** (100,000–): modern humans.

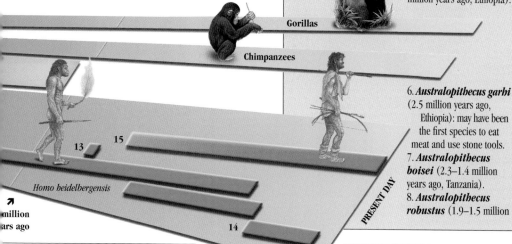

Gorillas

Chimpanzees

13 15

Homo heidelbergensis

PRESENT DAY

14

million ars ago

The peopling of the earth

There are different theories about how the earth was populated. According to the most widely accepted theory, early humans first appeared in Africa and migrated from there to populate the various parts of the globe. There were two migrations from Africa; the first took place around one million years ago when bands of *Homo erectus* spread across Europe and Asia. Their descendents all became extinct. Modern humans are all part of the same species – *Homo sapiens sapiens* (meaning "wise man") – which migrated from Africa around 100,000 years ago. They spread across the globe gradually. New Zealand, in the South Pacific, was one of the last places in the world to be inhabited – its original Maori inhabitants made the long journey across the Pacific Ocean in canoes about 1,000 years ago.

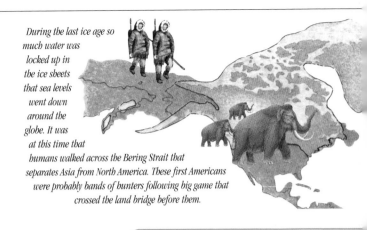

During the last ice age so much water was locked up in the ice sheets that sea levels went down around the globe. It was at this time that humans walked across the Bering Strait that separates Asia from North America. These first Americans were probably bands of hunters following big game that crossed the land bridge before them.

The mastery of fire

Homo erectus (1.7–250,000 years ago) appears to have been the first hominid to master the use of fire. This was a major technological breakthrough that greatly improved the quality of hominid life. Fire provided warmth and, along with the invention of clothing and shelter, helped *Homo erectus* survive in the much colder climates outside of tropical Africa. Fire was also used for cooking meat, which made it more digestible and beneficial because heat breaks down some of meat's more complex compounds. But perhaps the greatest benefit from fire was the protection it offered against wild animals. Early humans were often attacked at night by carnivores such as lions or saber-toothed tigers. These ferocious animals were afraid of fire and kept a safe distance.

The importance of climate

The earth's climate changed quite dramatically many times during prehistory. During the Pleistocene epoch (1.6 million to 10,000 years ago), there were a series of ice ages. During the biggest ice age more than 30 percent of the earth's surface was covered in ice sheets (compared with about 10 percent today). The extreme cold must have made conditions very hard for our ancestors, although by lowering sea levels it made it possible for them to walk between land areas that are now separated by seas, thus helping them spread over the earth's surface.

SCANDINAVIA
12,000 years ago

SIBERIA
30,000 years ago

CZECH REPUBLIC
33,000 years ago

CHINA
67,000 years ago

ASIA

JAPAN
30,000 years ago

AFRICA

INDIAN OCEAN

Area of human origins

AUSTRALIA
50,000 years

This trail of footprints (right) was left in volcanic ash by a group of early humans over 3.6 million years ago in Laetoli, Tanzania.

Increasing brain size

Fossils of hominid brain cases show the increasing sizes of the brains they contained. Although hominid bodies also increased in size and weight, brain size increased at a much faster pace. At 256–315 cubic inches (650–800 cubic centimeters) the brain of *Homo habilis* was larger than that of the australopithecenes 177–217 ci (450–550 cc). This increase in brain size probably coincided with the invention of stone tools. Modern humans' brains are almost twice the size as that of *Homo habilis*. See the diagram (right) for relative brain sizes.

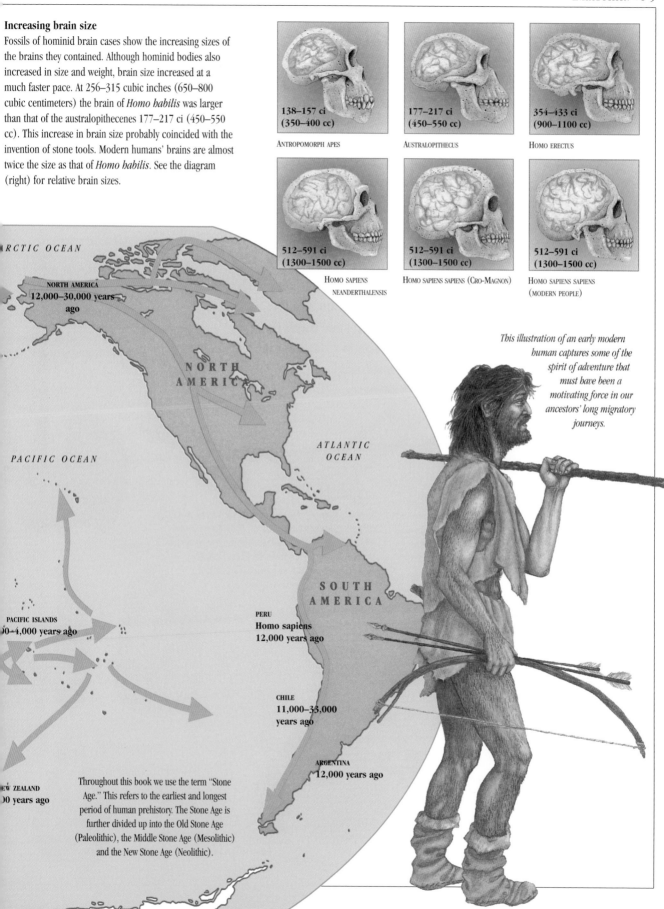

138–157 ci (350–400 cc)
ANTROPOMORPH APES

177–217 ci (450–550 cc)
AUSTRALOPITHECUS

354–433 ci (900–1100 cc)
HOMO ERECTUS

512–591 ci (1300–1500 cc)
HOMO SAPIENS NEANDERTHALENSIS

512–591 ci (1300–1500 cc)
HOMO SAPIENS SAPIENS (CRO-MAGNON)

512–591 ci (1300–1500 cc)
HOMO SAPIENS SAPIENS (MODERN PEOPLE)

This illustration of an early modern human captures some of the spirit of adventure that must have been a motivating force in our ancestors' long migratory journeys.

ARCTIC OCEAN

NORTH AMERICA
12,000–30,000 years ago

NORTH AMERICA

PACIFIC OCEAN

ATLANTIC OCEAN

SOUTH AMERICA

PACIFIC ISLANDS
00–4,000 years ago

PERU
Homo sapiens
12,000 years ago

CHILE
11,000–33,000 years ago

ARGENTINA
12,000 years ago

EW ZEALAND
00 years ago

Throughout this book we use the term "Stone Age." This refers to the earliest and longest period of human prehistory. The Stone Age is further divided up into the Old Stone Age (Paleolithic), the Middle Stone Age (Mesolithic) and the New Stone Age (Neolithic).

The Invention of Tools

The development of tools was an extremely slow and gradual process. The first hominids probably used pointed sticks or sharp-edged bones, shells and stones to probe for insects or cut into the flesh of animals they scavenged or caught. The earliest intentionally made tools found so far date to around 2.5 million years ago. Known as "choppers," they are fist-sized rocks from which one end has been chipped away to make a roughly serrated edge for cutting. Other tools gradually appeared and by around 100,000 years ago humans had developed a whole range of new ones, including hand axes, knives, borers and spears. These were followed by burins, which were strong, narrow-bladed flints used to carve bone into needles and fishhooks. Later humans learned to fit handles on their tools and weapons, making them even more useful. By Neolithic times, they had learned to grind stone blades to make axes with very sharp cutting edges that could be used to clear forests for agriculture.

Chopper

Hand axe

The first tools – choppers – were made by hitting a core stone or pebble with a hammerstone so that flakes of the core were removed to create a sharp cutting edge. The flakes could also be used for cutting. Only one end of the stone was chipped and the smooth and rounded section was held in the palm of the hand.

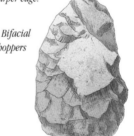

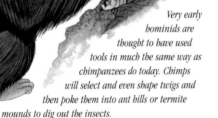

Very early hominids are thought to have used tools in much the same way as chimpanzees do today. Chimps will select and even shape twigs and then poke them into ant hills or termite mounds to dig out the insects.

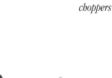

The manufacture of chopping tools slowly evolved, and by about 500,000 years ago hominids had discovered that they could use a softer material, such as bone, antler or wood, to chip off much smaller flakes to make a chopper or hand ax with a much sharper edge.

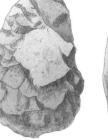

Scrapers

Bifacial choppers

Pointed hand axe

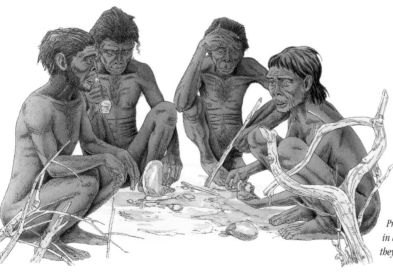

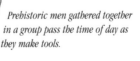

Prehistoric men gathered together in a group pass the time of day as they make tools.

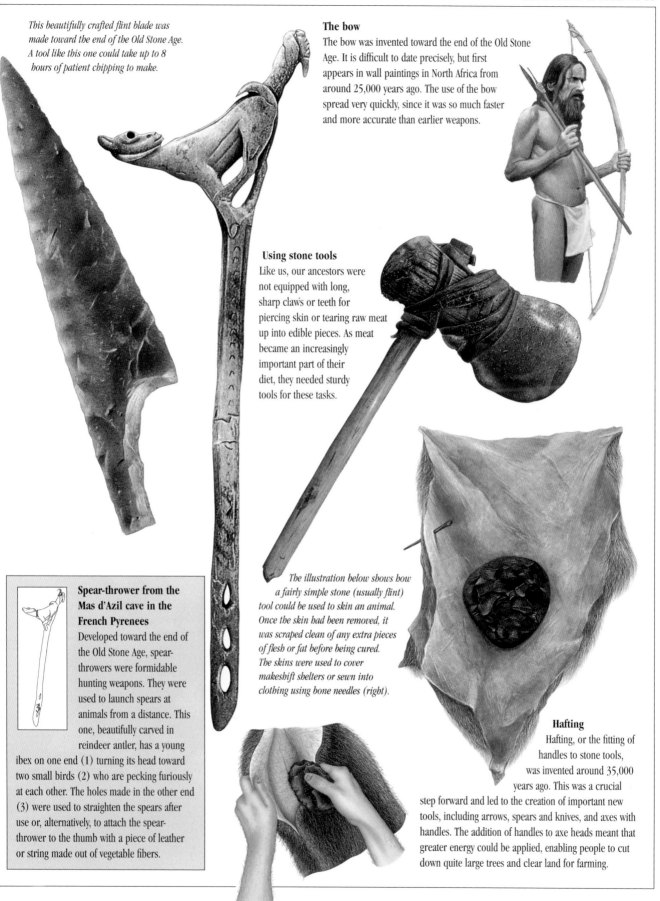

This beautifully crafted flint blade was made toward the end of the Old Stone Age. A tool like this one could take up to 8 hours of patient chipping to make.

The bow

The bow was invented toward the end of the Old Stone Age. It is difficult to date precisely, but first appears in wall paintings in North Africa from around 25,000 years ago. The use of the bow spread very quickly, since it was so much faster and more accurate than earlier weapons.

Using stone tools

Like us, our ancestors were not equipped with long, sharp claws or teeth for piercing skin or tearing raw meat up into edible pieces. As meat became an increasingly important part of their diet, they needed sturdy tools for these tasks.

The illustration below shows how a fairly simple stone (usually flint) tool could be used to skin an animal. Once the skin had been removed, it was scraped clean of any extra pieces of flesh or fat before being cured. The skins were used to cover makeshift shelters or sewn into clothing using bone needles (right).

Spear-thrower from the Mas d'Azil cave in the French Pyrenees
Developed toward the end of the Old Stone Age, spear-throwers were formidable hunting weapons. They were used to launch spears at animals from a distance. This one, beautifully carved in reindeer antler, has a young ibex on one end (1) turning its head toward two small birds (2) who are pecking furiously at each other. The holes made in the other end (3) were used to straighten the spears after use or, alternatively, to attach the spear-thrower to the thumb with a piece of leather or string made out of vegetable fibers.

Hafting

Hafting, or the fitting of handles to stone tools, was invented around 35,000 years ago. This was a crucial step forward and led to the creation of important new tools, including arrows, spears and knives, and axes with handles. The addition of handles to axe heads meant that greater energy could be applied, enabling people to cut down quite large trees and clear land for farming.

Hunters and Gatherers

Until about 10,000 years ago people lived by scavenging, hunting and fishing and by gathering the plants, roots, seeds, nuts and fruit that grew wild in their surroundings.

The earliest humans, such as *Homo habilis*, were small, slightly built creatures who, without the use of spears and bows, probably lived mainly on plant foods. What little meat they did eat would have been scavenged from the carcasses of animals that were already dead. Full-scale, active hunting came later, when larger-brained humans with better tools were forced by successive ice ages (when plant food was scarce) to become skillful hunters to survive. Hunters and gatherers were continually on the move as they followed prey or moved to areas where they knew that other food sources would be plentiful.

Gathering

It is difficult to know almost anything about how prehistoric gathering was done. Archaeologists have relied heavily on studies of the few remaining hunting and gathering societies to understand how earlier groups lived. They think that women and children were responsible for finding roots, grains, seeds, fruit, insects and small animals, which they carried back to the camp for everyone to share.

This rock painting (near left) from Spain shows a woman dangling from a cliff face as she gathers honey. The tiny figure on the far left comes from a rock painting and shows a man using a lasso.

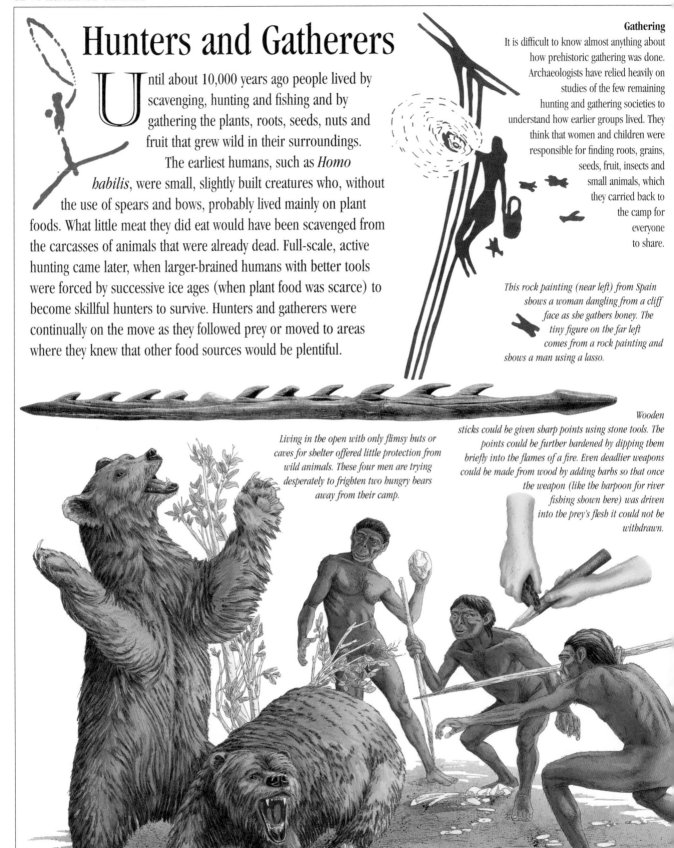

Wooden sticks could be given sharp points using stone tools. The points could be further hardened by dipping them briefly into the flames of a fire. Even deadlier weapons could be made from wood by adding barbs so that once the weapon (like the harpoon for river fishing shown here) was driven into the prey's flesh it could not be withdrawn.

Living in the open with only flimsy huts or caves for shelter offered little protection from wild animals. These four men are trying desperately to frighten two hungry bears away from their camp.

This 20th-century hunter-gatherer from Southeast Asia has used a stick to poke ants out of their nest. Ants are considered a tasty treat by some tribal people today, just as they must have been for early humans.

The importance of memory

Hunter-gatherer groups returned at regular intervals to the same places. They learned where good food and water could be found and this information was passed down from generation to generation.

A few of the San people, hunters and gatherers of the Kalahari Desert in southern Africa, live today much as their ancestors did. Well-adapted to life in the desert, they know all its secrets, including where to find essential water.

Versatile tastes

Early humans, like modern ones, were versatile feeders and could survive on diets that varied widely according to the season and what was available. The ability to switch from one food source to another is one of the reasons why humans have been so successful; animals that can only feed on one type of food can die out if that food becomes rare or disappears.

Deadly hunters

As early humans became more intelligent they became increasingly deadly hunters. Working in a group, they could bring down even the largest prey, such as woolly mammoths. They could also learn animals' habits, for example that they came to the watering hole in the evening or followed certain routes according to the season, and lie in wait. Even more crucially, as time went by they developed weapons, such as spears and arrows, which could be fired from afar so that they stayed at a safe distance from the terrified or wounded prey. Humans are the only hunters who are able to do this.

The bola (above), made of weighted rope, was whirled around the hunter's head and then thrown at game animals. The stone weights wrapped the rope around the animals' legs, bringing them to the ground.

The deer hunters

This reconstruction is based on a rock painting from Valtorta in Spain (now illegible). It shows four archers (1) as they shoot their arrows (2) at a group of deer. The deer have been carefully depicted: there are two stags (3), one of which is quite young judging by its small antlers; six does (4), and two fawns (5).

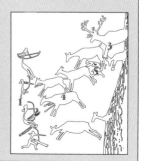

Burials and Beliefs

Humans began to make special graves for people after they had died during the middle of the Old Stone Age (c. 80,000–35,000 years ago). Burial is seen as a major step forward for humans because it implies that they believed in a soul or in life after death (or both). These are complex ideas that go beyond the worries of day-to-day survival and may suggest the beginnings of religious beliefs.

In many early burials, the body was lain on one side, often with the legs drawn up.

A rich store of information

Burials provide a wealth of information about people from ancient times, such as how they lived, the diseases they suffered, what they died of, their state of health, and much more. Teeth can reveal a lot about diet, while stomach contents can help us understand what people ate.

The burial

The way the body has been treated is important. Bodies could be simply buried in the soil, cremated, made into mummies, or even cut into pieces. In many cases the body was decorated with shells or flowers before burial. The Menton man, shown here, was covered in small sea shells and pierced animal teeth.

Grave goods

Many ancient tombs contain pots, bowls, jewelry, weapons, clothing, food and many other objects. These items, known as "grave goods," were probably placed in the tomb to help the dead person in their next life. Archaeologists can learn a lot about the wealth and status of the person buried by studying these. A very rich or royal person usually had many beautiful goods in their tombs, while a poorer person might only have a few simple items. Children were sometimes buried with their toys.

These animal teeth were found in a grave in southern France. They are all pierced and were probably strung together as a necklace.

This mummy was found in Peru. It contains the remains of an Inca man who was about 35 years old when he died more than 1,500 years ago. His rich cloak of feathers, serpent mouthpiece, golden crown and other ornaments suggest that he was very wealthy, perhaps even a king or prince.

A man at Dolní Vestonice in the Czech Republic was buried wearing this shell necklace during the last ice age.

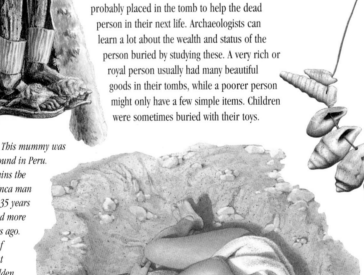

The discovery of a tomb at Mallaha, in Israel, where a puppy was placed in a boy's arms, helped archaeologists understand that dogs were probably the first animals to be tamed. Even before the development of agriculture, wild dogs may have learned to hang around campsites where they could scavenge food and where puppies could have been tamed by children. Although we will never know what really happened, burials show that by at least 11,000 years ago dogs already occupied a place within family life, much as they do today.

Early religion

Without written records it is very difficult to tell what prehistoric humans believed. However, some rock paintings and evidence of ceremonies performed when burying the dead suggest that from some time in the Middle Stone Age *Homo sapiens* and Neanderthals both held some kind of religious beliefs.

Reconstruction of a figure known as "the Sorcerer" from the Trois Frères cave in France. It has a mixture of animal and human features.

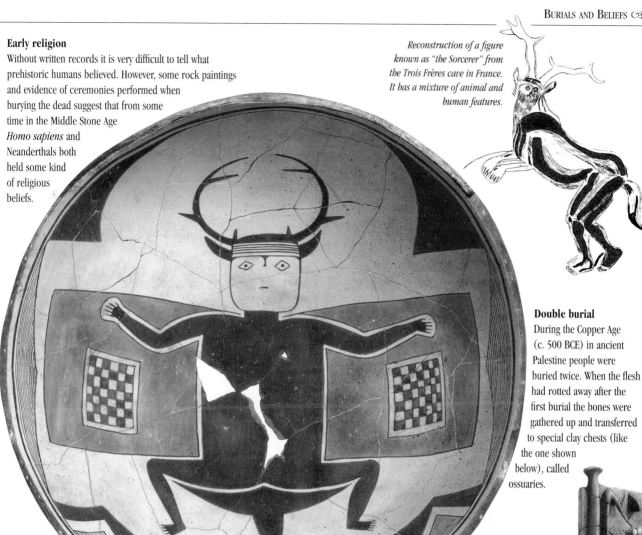

Double burial

During the Copper Age (c. 500 BCE) in ancient Palestine people were buried twice. When the flesh had rotted away after the first burial the bones were gathered up and transferred to special clay chests (like the one shown below), called ossuaries.

Mimbres pottery bowls

The Mimbres people lived in prehistoric New Mexico, USA. About 1,000 years ago Mimbres potters created magnificent painted ceremonial bowls. These were placed in tombs, usually upside down over the dead person's head. This bowl shows a creature with the face (1), hands (2) and feet (3) of a human, the antlers (4) of a deer and the wings (5) of a bat. This probably refers to the way shamans were thought to be transformed into animals during their ritual dances. The bowls have holes in the middle (6), made to "kill" the object, helping release the vessel's spirit into the next world.

During Neolithic (New Stone Age) times in Jericho the skull was often separated from the rest of the skeleton. It was then covered with plaster, like the one shown here. Sometimes shells were placed in the eye sockets. These remodelled heads may have been used for ancestor worship.

Art and Crafts

Prehistoric people have left us a variety of art forms, including cave paintings, engravings and sculptures. The beautiful cave paintings are perhaps the most striking of all. It was *Homo sapiens* who first decorated caves, starting around 35,000 years ago. The first artists mainly depicted large game animals, such as woolly mammoths, bison, deer, wild horses and oxen. Only later, from around 12,000 years ago, did the human figure appear. Still rare, it was usually shown in hunting or livestock scenes. Everywhere, from the earliest times, abstract drawings (patterns with no humans, animals or plants) abound; these are sometimes interpreted as simple doodles or primitive counting methods, and sometimes as territorial markings, early forms of land register, or even as plans of houses and views of buildings.

The origins of art are lost in the very distant past. We don't know when our ancestors began to make, or even to recognize, objects that were more than just useful. The water-worn ironstone cobble above was found in a cave in South Africa inhabited by australopithecines 3 million years ago. They carried it for at least 20 miles (32 km) to their cave dwelling, presumably because it looked like a human face.

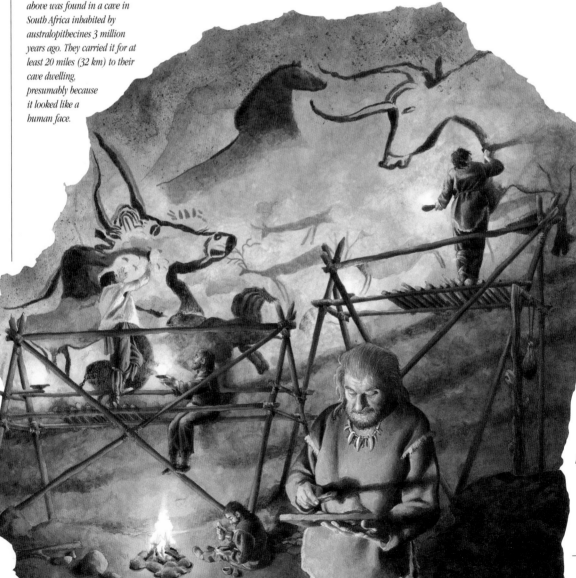

Artists working inside dark caves used flaming torches or stone lamps that burnt animal fat to light the walls and ceilings on which they worked. The carved lamp from Lascaux (opposite) is a rare example of a more elaborate lighting device.

In order to reach the highest parts of the cave, the artists may have either used a pole, with a "brush" tied to the end of it, or built scaffolding on which to stand (as shown in our reconstruction).

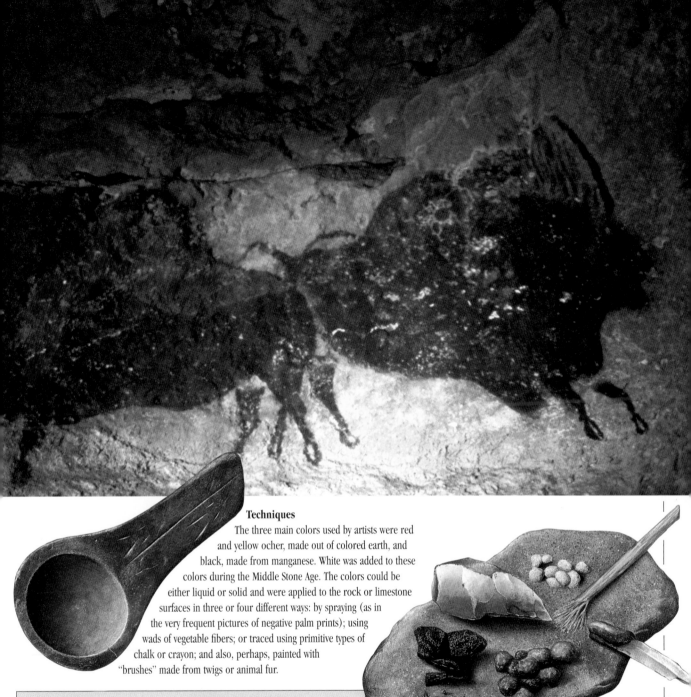

Techniques

The three main colors used by artists were red and yellow ocher, made out of colored earth, and black, made from manganese. White was added to these colors during the Middle Stone Age. The colors could be either liquid or solid and were applied to the rock or limestone surfaces in three or four different ways: by spraying (as in the very frequent pictures of negative palm prints); using wads of vegetable fibers; or traced using primitive types of chalk or crayon; and also, perhaps, painted with "brushes" made from twigs or animal fur.

Painted bison at Lascaux

This powerful painting is a fine example of the prehistoric painters' technical and artistic ability. The bison (1 and 2), which have probably just finished fighting, are galloping off in opposite directions. Both animals, portrayed using foreshortening, are not only depicted in outline; the huge weight of their powerful bodies is conveyed by expanses of red and black coloring that round out their shapes. The artists have also rendered the idea of depth and perspective: the back legs (3) of the bison on the right are not aligned with those of the other animal, but are slightly higher, as dictated by the rules of spatial depth and distance perspective. The same applies to the back of the right-hand bison (4), which can be seen over and above the back of the bison on the left.

Our reconstruction of a prehistoric painter's "palette" shows a selection of the instruments and colors used. The wooden "brush" was used to apply the colors, while the charcoal in the foreground was applied directly to the rock. The other minerals were crushed into powder form and then mixed with water before use.

The Mother Goddess

Some of the earliest works of art were tiny statues of women. Dating from about 25,000 years ago, they were probably used as fertility symbols in religious ceremonies. Later they became associated with the Mother Goddess, the center of life and the family, and an object of worship in central and southern Europe and in the Near East throughout the Neolithic and Bronze ages.

Rock art

As well as cave paintings, prehistoric people also painted and engraved on rocks. Examples of rock art have survived from around the world.

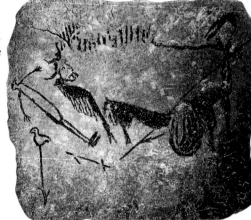

Rock painting from Lascaux showing a wounded bison with its entrails hanging out.

Below: A mystical figure from the Tassili Massif in the central Sahara.

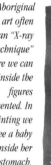 *Right: Aboriginal rock art often uses an "X-ray technique" where we can see inside the figures represented. In this painting we can see a baby inside her mother's stomach.*

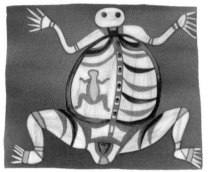

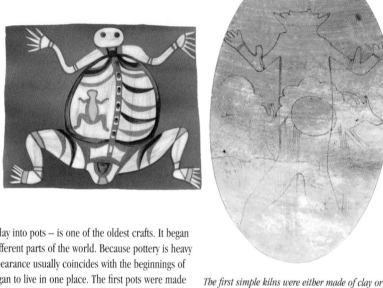

Below: The first pottery in the world was made by people of the Jomon culture in Japan beginning around 13,000 years ago. This pointed Jamon pot is from the early period.

Pottery

Pottery – the making of clay into pots – is one of the oldest crafts. It began independently in many different parts of the world. Because pottery is heavy and easy to break, its appearance usually coincides with the beginnings of farming, when people began to live in one place. The first pots were made by coiling strips of clay around a solid base. Decorations were then painted or scratched onto the sides before the pots were fired briefly over an open fire. Early forms of the potter's wheel were in use by about 5,500 years ago. Special kilns to fire the pots at high temperatures, making them watertight, also appeared at an early date.

The first simple kilns were either made of clay or dug into the ground (like the one shown here). They consisted of two chambers – the lower one, where a wood fire was built, and an upper one, where the pots were placed for firing.

Kiln chamber

Flue

Firing chamber

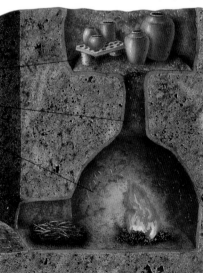

Glazed and painted pot from the Yangshao culture in China (c. 3100–1700 BCE).

Portable art and statues

As well as cave paintings and rock art, people also began to develop smaller pieces of art that could be carried around with them on their frequent journeys. Tiny carvings and statues of animals and female figures were among the most common types.

This gazelle-shaped sickle handle was carved from bone by people of the Natufian culture in Palestine during the Middle Stone Age.

Right: The Olmecs, founders of Central America's oldest civilization, were master sculptors. Using only the simplest of tools, they carved volcanic rock into huge statues of heads and altars. They also cut harder stone into miniature works of art, like the baby figure shown here.

Spinning and weaving

The ability to spin and weave plant and animal fibers to make clothing made it possible for humans to survive in cold climates. This helped them spread across the globe. The first cloth, made in Mesopotamia about 6500 BCE, was spun from linen. The Chinese began to make silk about 5,000 years ago. After people had domesticated sheep, goats and camels, they soon found that their hair could be spun into fine yarn and then woven into warm, hardwearing cloth.

This piece of decorated cloth was woven from linen in predynastic Egypt, over 5,000 years ago.

People began to make cloth in South America over 3,000 years ago. The shaman figure (above), from Peru, was made about 1200 BCE.

The mastery of metals

People discovered that metals can be made by applying heat to certain types of rock about 9,000 years ago. Once the metal had been smelted from the rock, it could be hammered or molded into tough, long-lasting tools, weapons and artifacts. The discovery of metal was a great technological breakthrough that gave people far greater control over their surroundings. The discovery was so important that archaeologists now date late prehistoric times into the Copper, Bronze or Iron ages, according to the metal used.

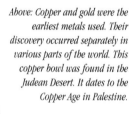

Above: Copper and gold were the earliest metals used. Their discovery occurred separately in various parts of the world. This copper bowl was found in the Judean Desert. It dates to the Copper Age in Palestine.

Bronze statue of an elephant made during the Shang Dynasty in China.

Right: Simple shell and seed necklaces from the Middle East and Egypt, plus some very early gold earrings, made in Palestine.

Jewelry

The wearing of ornaments and jewelry began in the Old Stone Age, about 30,000 years ago. The earliest jewelry was made from shells, seeds, teeth, feathers, bones and other items that could be made into decorative objects and worn. Brightly colored stones, such as lapiz lazuli, jade and turquoise, and precious metals, including gold and silver, began to be used during Neolithic times. The desire to own beautiful jewels encouraged the growth of trade as precious stones and metals were exchanged across ever expanding frontiers.

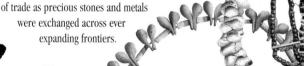

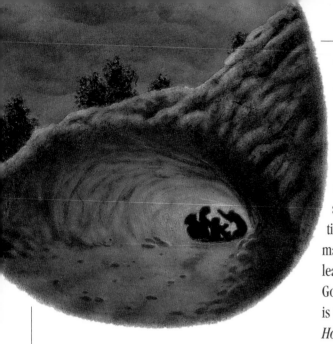

Early Homes

Prehistoric humans are sometimes called "cave men" because it is thought that they all lived in caves. This is only partly true; while some early humans did inhabit caves, many more are known to have lived in cave mouths, rock shelters and a wide variety of open-air dwellings. From very early times our ancestors knew how to build simple huts and tents using many different materials, including stone, wood, branches and leaves, and the hides, and even the bones, of animals. In the Olduvai Gorge (Tanzania), for example, a circle of stones was found that is thought to have marked the base of a brushwood hut built by *Homo habilis* around 1.8 million years ago.

Caves

This illustration shows a group of *Homo erectus* gathered around a fire deep inside a limestone cave at Zhoukoudian, in China. For a long time these caves were believed to have been permanent homes for *Homo erectus* for around 200,000 years, from 460,000 BCE onward. Recently, some scholars have pointed out that dark, damp, often slippery and rocky caverns would not have been the most comfortable of dwellings and that people may only have stayed in them temporarily when conditions outside were either extremely cold or hot. We do know that people lived in the mouths of caves, where they had shelter but avoided the darkness and dampness within.

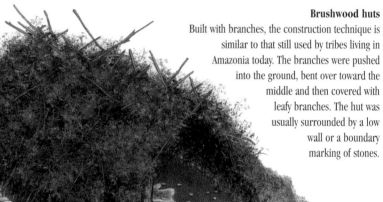

A row of stones have been placed around the hut as a boundary marker.

Brushwood huts

Built with branches, the construction technique is similar to that still used by tribes living in Amazonia today. The branches were pushed into the ground, bent over toward the middle and then covered with leafy branches. The hut was usually surrounded by a low wall or a boundary marking of stones.

Portable tents

Tents that could be taken down and carried along with the rest of the group's possessions were another type of prehistoric dwelling. They had a wooden frame and were covered with animal skins to keep out the wind and the cold.

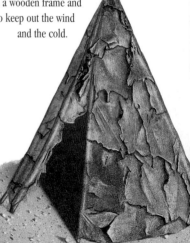

Rock shelters

An outcrop of rock facing into the sun made a convenient dwelling place. Holes could be pierced in the rock to hold wooden poles or thread ropes through to support a canopy made of animal skin or other materials. Inside there was a hearth, marked out by stones, straw pallet beds and a space set aside for work.

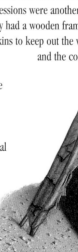

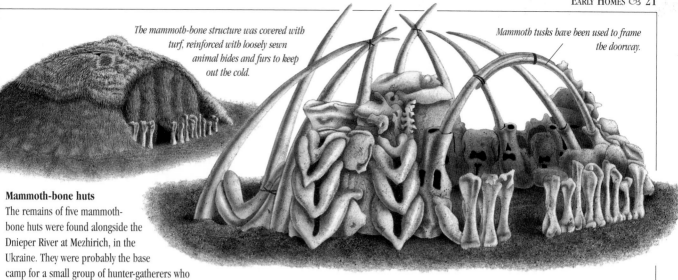

The mammoth-bone structure was covered with turf, reinforced with loosely sewn animal hides and furs to keep out the cold.

Mammoth tusks have been used to frame the doorway.

Mammoth-bone huts

The remains of five mammoth-bone huts were found alongside the Dnieper River at Mezhirich, in the Ukraine. They were probably the base camp for a small group of hunter-gatherers who traveled around the region. The huts all had hearths, work areas and a large amount of debris. They date to about 18,000 years ago.

Reconstruction of one of the shelters on the pebbly seashore at Terra Amata, in southern France. The carefully cut branches were fitted together tightly to break the wind and the perimeter was marked out by stones. There was a smoke hole in the top. Because Terra Amata dates to about 380,000 years ago, some scholars doubt that these early shelters were quite so complex.

This bone (left) has been both sculpted and engraved. The top part has been carved into the shape of a bird's head while a fish and a deer have been engraved on the lower part.

Detail from an engraved reindeer bone (left) from La Vache, which shows three large cats. The central figure (shown here) is bounding along energetically.

Cave dwellings

Alliat, an archaeological site in the French Pyrenees, was a cave dwelling used for about 500 years after 10,900 BCE. The tribal hearth was situated in the innermost area of the cave, out of reach of bad weather. Many works of art were found, mostly portable objects such as decorated bowls and carvings on reindeer bones. One of the cave's openings looks out across the valley toward the entrance to the Niaux cave where the inhabitants of La Vache performed dances and rites for hunting trips. They left behind an impressive series of paintings, mainly of animal figures.

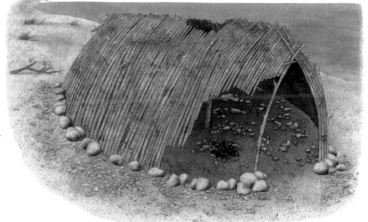

The hearth, where food was cooked and where people gathered for warmth, would have been the central hub of a prehistoric shelter.

This carved tool (below) has a salmon engraved on its surface. The elongated head may have been used as a scraper.

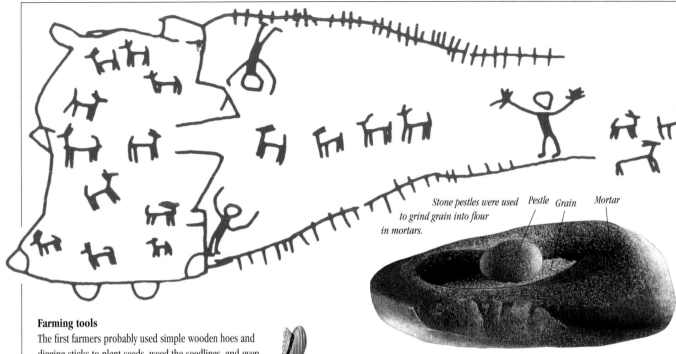

Stone pestles were used
to grind grain into flour
in mortars.

Pestle   Grain   Mortar

Farming tools

The first farmers probably used simple wooden hoes and
digging sticks to plant seeds, weed the seedlings, and even
harvest many of them. Cereal crops led to the invention of
the sickle, which consisted of a wooden handle with
pieces of flint inserted into it that was used to cut
grain. The plow, invented quite early in Europe
and Asia, did not spread beyond those areas until
modern times. Although the animals used to pull
it, usually cattle, were expensive to buy and
keep, the plow allowed much larger areas
of land to be cultivated, thus
producing greater harvests
and, ultimately, wealth.

*Reconstruction
of an early sickle.*

The Birth of Agriculture

The end of the last ice age around 10,000 years ago brought
considerable changes to the natural environment, including the
retreat of the ice cap, a rise in sea levels, abundant rainfall and
the growth of rich vegetation in areas formerly covered by ice. Game animals
became more plentiful and people moved north and south into regions that
had been too cold for humans for thousands of years. It was during this period
of revival and change that people gradually began to cultivate plants and raise
livestock and early farming began. Agriculture developed separately in very distant
parts of the world. Traces of the first farmers in the Near East date to about 10,000
years ago. Soon afterward, farming also appeared in China, Mexico and northern
India. Different plants and animals were domesticated in each of these areas: wheat,
barley, sheep and goats were typical of the Near East; rice and millet of Asia; and
maize, beans, potatoes and llamas
of the Americas. Agriculture soon
spread, gradually replacing the
earlier hunter-gatherer societies. As
farmers became more skilled they
were able to produce more food
and feed many more people. As
their small settled communities
grew, their houses clustered
together into villages and towns.

Bringing in the sheep

This typical farming scene shows
three men herding their animals
into an enclosure. It comes from
Ruyum, in Jordan, and dates to
Neolithic times. The long lines
crossed by the shorter ones (1)
represent a fenced corridor (2).
The man at the entrance to this (3) is waving his arms about to drive the animals (goats or sheep) toward
the entrance of the enclosure. Two more men (4 and 5) standing on either side of the entrance are making
the same gestures as the first man to herd the animals inside. Strangely, the artist has also shown three
animals behind the first man (6) who have apparently escaped his notice and are going free.

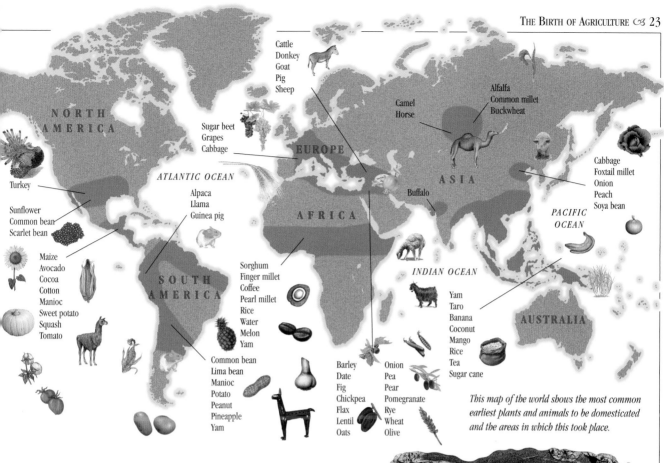

Cattle
Donkey
Goat
Pig
Sheep

Camel
Horse

Alfalfa
Common millet
Buckwheat

Sugar beet
Grapes
Cabbage

EUROPE

ASIA

Cabbage
Foxtail millet
Onion
Peach
Soya bean

Turkey

ATLANTIC OCEAN

Buffalo

PACIFIC
OCEAN

Sunflower
Common bean
Scarlet bean

Alpaca
Llama
Guinea pig

AFRICA

NORTH
AMERICA

Maize
Avocado
Cocoa
Cotton
Manioc
Sweet potato
Squash
Tomato

SOUTH
AMERICA

Sorghum
Finger millet
Coffee
Pearl millet
Rice
Water
Melon
Yam

INDIAN OCEAN

Yam
Taro
Banana
Coconut
Mango
Rice
Tea
Sugar cane

AUSTRALIA

Common bean
Lima bean
Manioc
Potato
Peanut
Pineapple
Yam

Barley
Date
Fig
Chickpea
Flax
Lentil
Oats

Onion
Pea
Pear
Pomegranate
Rye
Wheat
Olive

This map of the world shows the most common earliest plants and animals to be domesticated and the areas in which this took place.

The domestication of plants

Plants were first domesticated in areas that lie in the tropical and subtropical zones just to the north and south of the equator (see map above). Some plants were domesticated independently in more than one area. The first domestic plants would have been much smaller and had much lower yields than the ones we know today. Early farmers, like modern ones, managed the reproduction of their plants to increase yields by selecting the largest and best strains for seeding.

The rock painting below comes from Jabbaren, in the Sahara Desert. Dating to about 4000 BCE, it depicts early herders driving two different types of cattle. It shows that a farming lifestyle had already appeared in North Africa by that time.

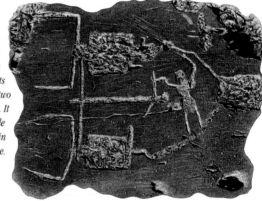

This sandstone engraving (above) from the Valcamonica in the Italian Alps, shows a bird's eye view of a plowman and his plow being drawn by two long-horned oxen.

The domestication of animals

Wild sheep and goats lived in central and western Asia. They are believed to have been domesticated first in western Asia. Wild ancestors of pigs and cattle lived throughout Europe and Asia and were probably domesticated separately at different times. Although there were fewer animals to domesticate in the Americas, llamas and alpacas soon became very important as pack animals and for their woolly coats.

Thick-wooled longhorn sheep on a vase from ancient Mesopotamia.

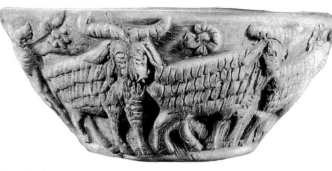

This terracotta vase was made by Olmec craftspeople over 3,000 years ago. The vase has a hole in the left knee for pouring liquids and was probably used by priests during religious ceremonies.

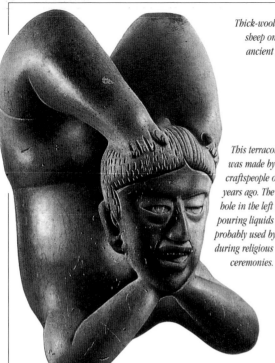

Mesopotamia

Farming villages appeared on the plains between the Tigris and Euphrates rivers (an area known as Mesopotamia, meaning "between the rivers") about 8,000 years ago. Mesopotamian farmers developed an effective irrigation system to water the arid plains. They produced more food than they could eat and traded the excess abroad. By about 5,500 years ago cities grew up in the south, in an area called Sumer. These were the first cities in the world.

From Village to City

By about 7,000 years ago farming villages were flourishing in the Middle East, the Nile Valley, northern China, the Indus Valley (in India), and in parts of Europe and Central and South America. As they became more efficient at producing food the villages grew in size and population. Their social organization gradually began to change as some people were freed from farming duties to become craftworkers and shopkeepers. Over time, trading links were established, and these gradually produced even more wealth. Many villages grew into towns and a few of them became cities, with wealthy priest-kings and a small court ruling over a large population of mostly poor craftspeople and farmers. It was in these cities that writing was first invented and prehistory came to an end.

Low relief carving of a Chavín warrior holding a battle axe, from Peru.

NORTH AMERICA

MEXICO

ATLANTIC OCEAN

PACIFIC OCEAN

SOUTH AMERICA

PERU

Central America and the Andes

The development of agriculture and, subsequently, of towns and cities, occurred slightly later in the Americas than in Europe and Asia. Farming began in present-day Mexico and in the Andes. Maize was the most important crop in these areas. Farming villages gradually appeared, located near the fields cultivated by the villagers. The villages all built temples and supported a group of priests. Some towns grew in size and power and by about 3,200 years ago the first two civilizations had appeared. These were the Olmecs in Mexico and the Chavín in the Andes.

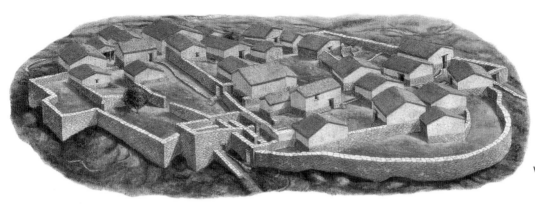

Europe

Farming spread to Europe from the Near East. It took hold first in the Balkans in southern Europe and then spread gradually westward. The fertile soils of Europe were well-suited to agriculture. Cattle and pigs were the main animals, while cereals were the most important crops.

The illustration shows a reconstruction of the farming village of Sesklo, in Greece. Established almost 8,000 years ago, this is one of the oldest villages in Europe. The rectangular houses were made of mud bricks and had thatched roofs. The village was surrounded by thick stone walls as protection against attacks from outside.

Reconstruction of the Neolithic farming village of Banpo, in northern China. The houses were square, round or oblong, with plastered floors. The village was surrounded by a ditch beyond which lay a pottery-making center with six kilns.

China

Many sites in northern China show that farming was well established in the region by around 8,000 years ago. Millet was grown, pigs and dogs were kept as domestic animals, and houses had special rooms for grain storage. The evidence also shows that rice cultivation in paddy fields was underway by about 6,000 years ago. Soon afterward the Yangshao and Longshan cultural groups began producing beautifully decorated pottery and jade objects that were probably used as items of exchange as trading grew and flourished. This prepared the way for the powerful Shang Dynasty, the first great civilization in China.

India

Farming began in northern India and Pakistan around 8,000 years ago. The first farming villages with mud brick houses appeared here. Centuries later, around 4,500 years ago, the first cities grew up in the Indus Valley. The two largest cities, Mohenjo-Daro and Harappa, each measured almost 3 miles (4.8 km) in circumference, and included a fortified citadel and a lower town.

Statue of a god or priest-king from the city of Mohenjo-Daro, in the Indus Valley.

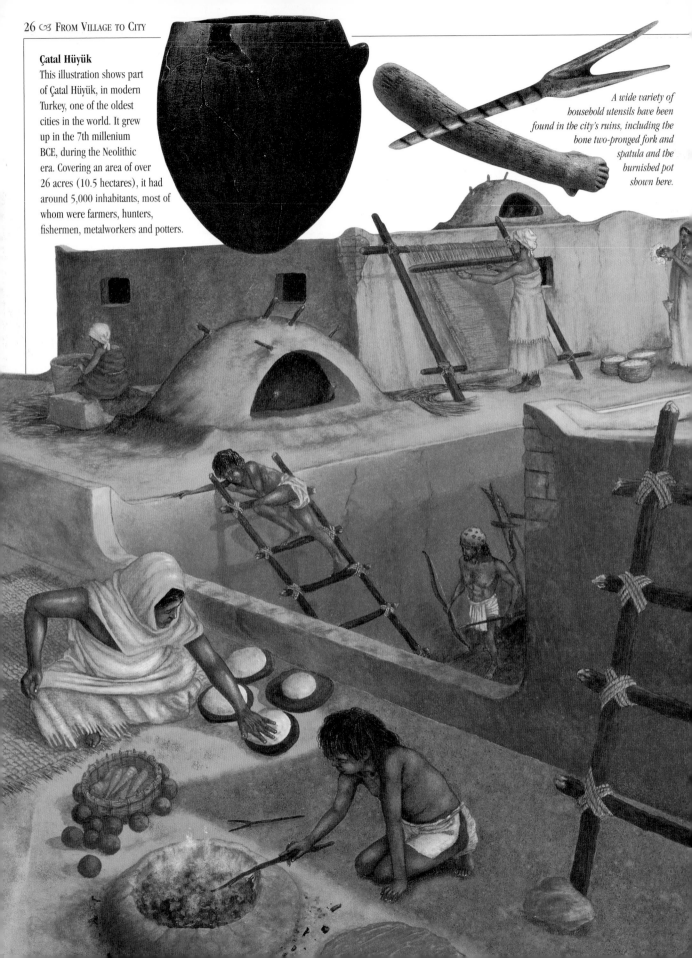

Çatal Hüyük
This illustration shows part of Çatal Hüyük, in modern Turkey, one of the oldest cities in the world. It grew up in the 7th millenium BCE, during the Neolithic era. Covering an area of over 26 acres (10.5 hectares), it had around 5,000 inhabitants, most of whom were farmers, hunters, fishermen, metalworkers and potters.

A wide variety of household utensils have been found in the city's ruins, including the bone two-pronged fork and spatula and the burnished pot shown here.

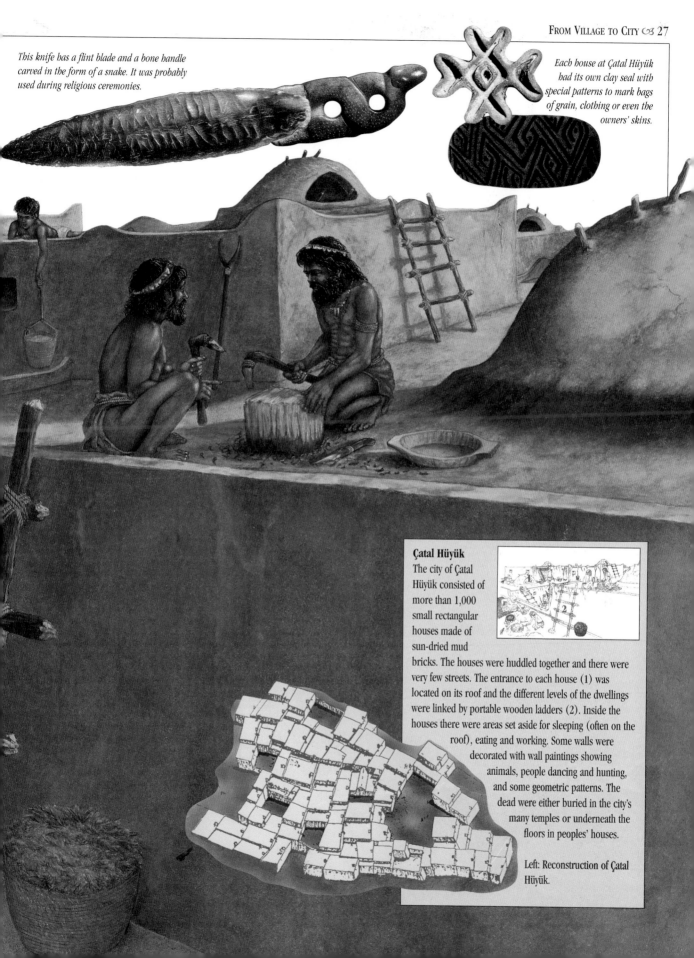

This knife has a flint blade and a bone handle carved in the form of a snake. It was probably used during religious ceremonies.

Each house at Çatal Hüyük had its own clay seal with special patterns to mark bags of grain, clothing or even the owners' skins.

Çatal Hüyük

The city of Çatal Hüyük consisted of more than 1,000 small rectangular houses made of sun-dried mud bricks. The houses were huddled together and there were very few streets. The entrance to each house (1) was located on its roof and the different levels of the dwellings were linked by portable wooden ladders (2). Inside the houses there were areas set aside for sleeping (often on the roof), eating and working. Some walls were decorated with wall paintings showing animals, people dancing and hunting, and some geometric patterns. The dead were either buried in the city's many temples or underneath the floors in peoples' houses.

Left: Reconstruction of Çatal Hüyük.

Stone Architecture

This dolmen (flat-topped stone tomb) stands at Bari, in southern Italy. Like others of its kind, it consists of a parallel line of upright stones, fully or partially covered by other large slabs of stone. Dolmen were usually collective tombs (with more than one body).

arming spread to north and western Europe very gradually and did not take root until several thousand years after its appearance in the Near East. Almost nothing remains of the early farming villages, which were probably built from perishable materials, such as timber and turf. However, these early European farmers did leave us an astonishing array of the huge stone monuments, called "megaliths" (from the Greek *megas* for "large" and *lithos* for "stone"). Excavations have revealed burials inside or near many of these monuments leading archaeologists to believe that they were used for burial ceremonies and other religious rituals. Some of the circular monuments, known as henges, have been built so that the first or last rays of the rising or setting sun strike the stones in a special way.

Stonehenge

An artist's reconstruction of Stonehenge as it looked during its final period in about 1100 BCE. The areas colored in light blue are no longer visible. Surrounded by a circular bank (1) and ditch (2), there were several inner circles of holes and standing stones. From the outside moving inward, these were: the Y holes (3), the Z holes (4), the Sarsen circle (5), the Bluestone circle (6), the Sarsen horseshoe (7), the Bluestone horseshoe (8) and the Altar stone (9). The North Barrow (10) and the South Barow (11) were flanked by Station stones (12). The roadway leading out of the circle, known as the Avenue (13), was marked at its beginning by the Slaughterstone (14) followed by the Heel Stone (15). We do not know precisely what happened at Stonehenge. However, like many other megalithic monuments, it was designed so that the sun rose and set in a particular spot during the midwinter and midsummer solstices. It seems probable that the farming communities gathered here on these occasions to celebrate the fertility of their lands and the changing of the seasons.

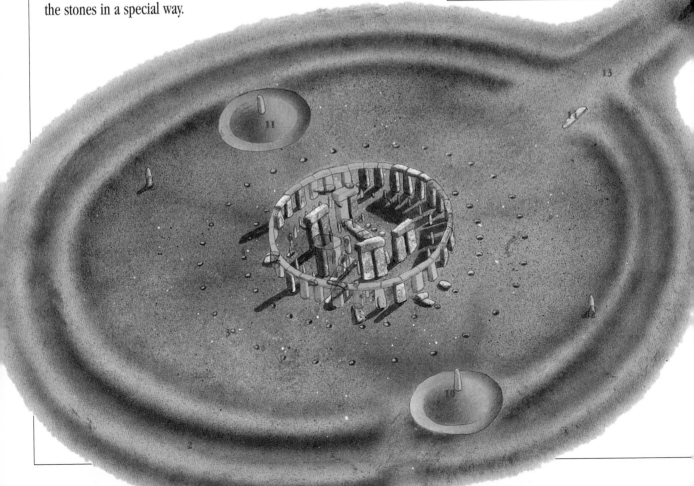

The beginnings

The first stone monuments, built from around 4500 BCE onward, were long barrows and megalithic tombs used for burials and ceremonies connected with the dead. The difficulties of building these monuments, using very heavy rocks that were often transported over long distances to the construction site, suggest that these Neolithic farming villages were closely knit, well-organized communities.

An international trend

Large stone monuments have been built in many different parts of the world over the centuries. Some megalithic tombs found in San Agustín in Colombia (right) contain monoliths carved into human figures with animal features to guard the peace of the dead. The early inhabitants of San Agustín believed that these enormous statues contained the spirits of the dead after they had been deprived of their original bodies.

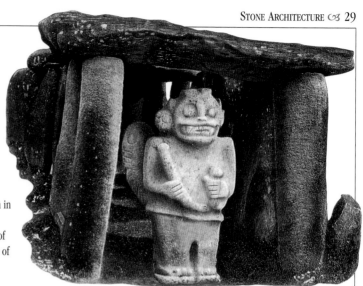

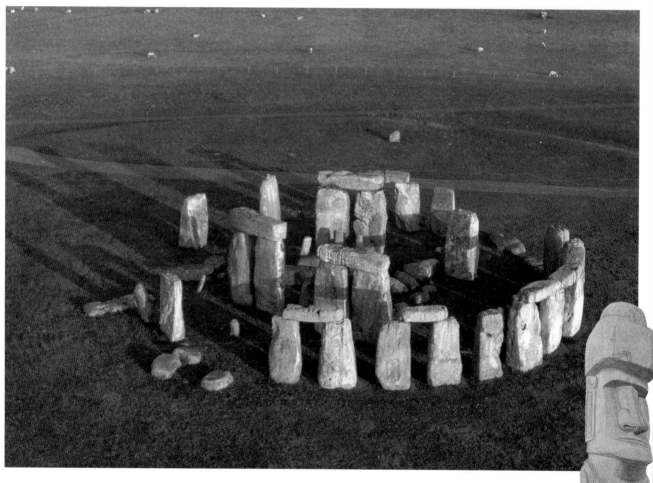

Above: Stonehenge as it looks today.

Stonehenge

Standing in the middle of the Salsbury Plain in England, Stonehenge is probably the best known megalithic monument in the world today. It was rebuilt several times over a period of about 2,000 years, between 5,100 and 3,100 years ago. It is one of more than 500 stone, wood and earthen monuments on the Salsbury Plain, which must have been a thriving religious and ceremonial center.

The towering megalithic figures on the Easter Islands were built over 1,000 years ago. Despite their relative youth, little is known about who built them or why.

Animals in Prehistory

B

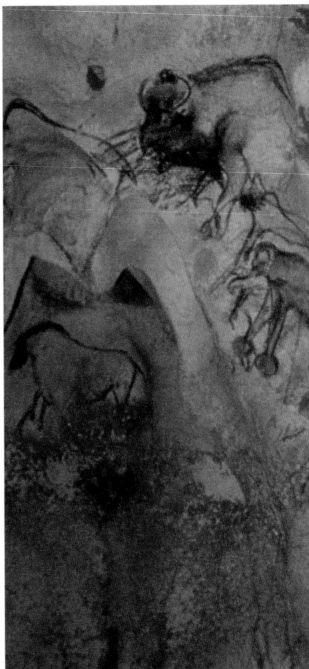

Animals were a primary food item and an important source of raw materials for tools and clothing from the earliest times. But as well as being of practical use, animals were important in other ways too. Prehistoric artists have left us a huge number of wall paintings, engravings and statues featuring animals. These works of art show us that early humans regarded them with mixed feelings of sympathy, awe, admiration and fear. Their lives were obviously clearly marked by their relationships with animals. What is striking about these works of art today is the abundance of animal life in prehistoric times and the number of species that have since died out.

A

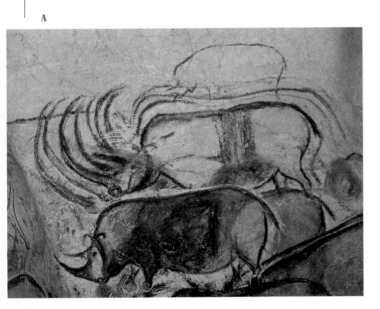

The Lion Panel (in the Chauvet Cave at Vallon Pont d'Arc, France)
Despite its name, this dynamic wall painting includes a wide variety of animals. The lions, and there are at least 13 of them, are on the right (1). They appear to be about to attack a herd of bison (2). In the left-hand section, a large number of rhinoceros (3) also seem to be trying to escape attack from the lions. The attention to detail and the information contained in this animated scene bring to mind a modern wildlife documentary. Almost as surprising as the great technical skill of the artist is the fact that all these animals, including the young mammoth with the ball-shaped hooves (4), should have been native to Europe at the time. Lions and rhinoceros are known to have disappeared from Europe during the last ice age, which reached its coldest point around 22,000 years ago.

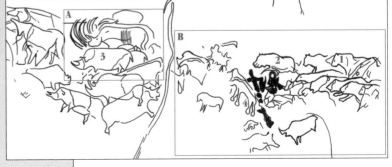

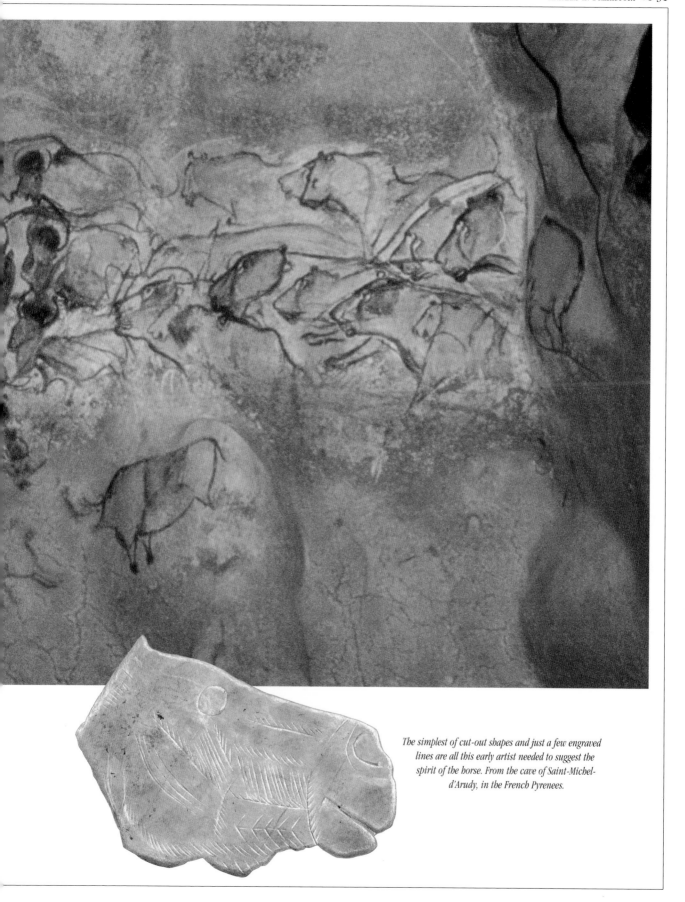

The simplest of cut-out shapes and just a few engraved lines are all this early artist needed to suggest the spirit of the horse. From the cave of Saint-Michel-d'Arudy, in the French Pyrenees.

Migration

Animals that now live in the
far north of Europe used to
live in central and
southern Europe during the
last ice age. With the retreat of the ice cap and the warming of
the earth, many favorite subjects of the cave artists of southern
Europe, such as the ibex and the reindeer, migrated north or
moved to the alps where it was always cold.

*Prehistoric hunters took care to preserve abundant
stocks of their preferred animals. They culled
more males than females, so that herd
numbers remained constant. Even so,
the changes in climate caused many
species, such as the giant
deer, to become extinct.*

*Prehistoric artists did not create realistic scenes, but grouped
animals of different species together according to
criteria of their own. We will never know why
these deer and salmon have been engraved
together on a reindeer horn.*

*The inquisitive face of a
hare appeared engraved into
stone at Isturitz, high in the Pyrenees
Mountains in Spain.*

*Sturdy spear-thrower carved from antler
and topped with a bird.*

*This pair of bison were
modelled in clay on the
floor of the cave of
Tuc d'Audobert, in
France. It is quite
unusual for a
prehistoric artist to
portray a group
scene.*

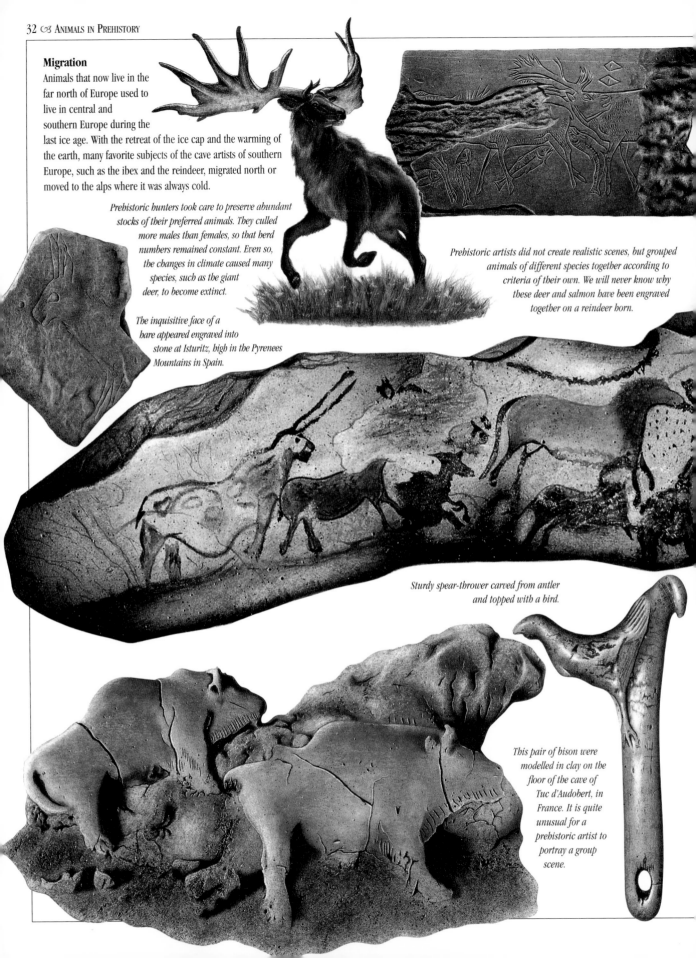

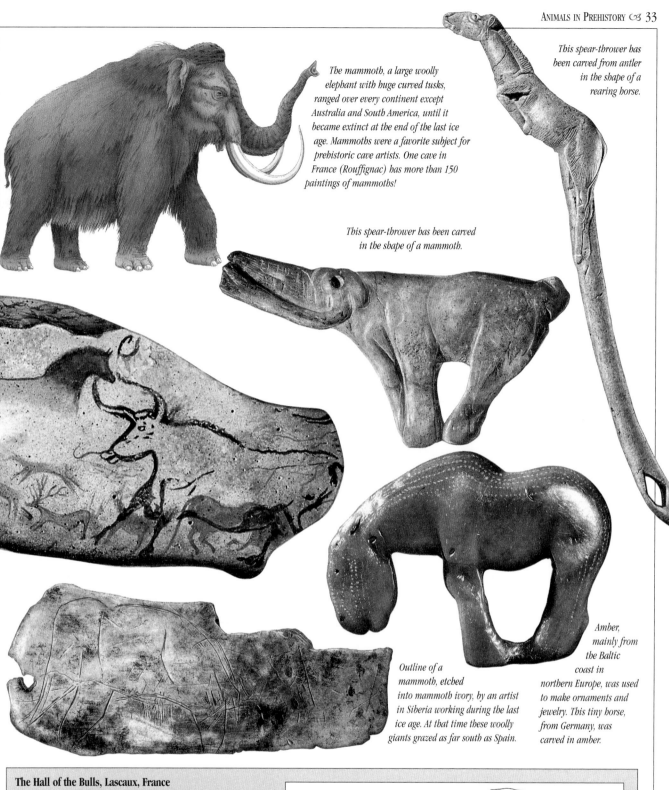

The mammoth, a large woolly elephant with huge curved tusks, ranged over every continent except Australia and South America, until it became extinct at the end of the last ice age. Mammoths were a favorite subject for prehistoric cave artists. One cave in France (Rouffignac) has more than 150 paintings of mammoths!

This spear-thrower has been carved from antler in the shape of a rearing horse.

This spear-thrower has been carved in the shape of a mammoth.

Outline of a mammoth, etched into mammoth ivory, by an artist in Siberia working during the last ice age. At that time these woolly giants grazed as far south as Spain.

Amber, mainly from the Baltic coast in northern Europe, was used to make ornaments and jewelry. This tiny horse, from Germany, was carved in amber.

The Hall of the Bulls, Lascaux, France

This reconstruction shows part of the Hall of the Bulls. Starting on the left, we see a mythical beast sometimes referred to as the "unicorn" (1), followed by horses (2) and a giant auroch (prehistoric ancestor of modern cattle) cow (3), all running toward the right where they will be met by an auroch bull (4). Between the two aurochs are a number of much smaller deer (5).

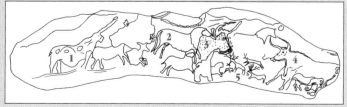

Dating the Past

During the 18th century many Europeans believed that the world had been created by God in 4004 BCE. They arrived at this date by making calculations based on the Bible. More scientifically minded people were only able to disprove this theory by accurately dating objects that are much older. Nowadays archaeologists use a range of different dating methods, depending on the age of the item they wish to date and the material of which it is made. Some methods, including the tree ring system, can give fairly precise dates even for objects from the distant past. Others, such as the Three Age system, provide relative "this before that" dating.

The Three Age system

With the passing of time human technology has become increasingly complex. As we have seen in this book, the first tools from over 2.5 million years ago were made from stone. This time up until the invention of bronze is known as the Stone Age. The time from the discovery of bronze to the invention of iron is known as the Bronze Age. The final period is known as the Iron Age. This is a relative dating method. A few societies in the modern world still have not discovered the use of bronze or iron.

This beautiful bronze head was made in Benin, in Africa, during the 15th century. The Bronze Age began much earlier in many other parts of the world, such as China and the Near East.

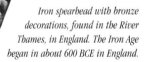

A superbly carved flint tool from the later part of the Stone Age in France. It dates to about 18,000 years ago.

Iron spearhead with bronze decorations, found in the River Thames, in England. The Iron Age began in about 600 BCE in England.

Tree ring dating

Tree ring dating, or dendrochronology, has been used to date objects made of wood since the 17th century. This method uses variations in the thickness of annual growth rings in tree trunks to date both living trees and items made from them. By piecing together overlapping growth ring patterns, scientists have created a chronology (timeline) that stretches back over 7,000 years.

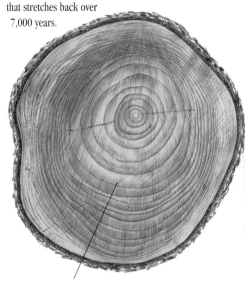

The thicker, paler part of the ring shows the growth the tree made during the summer, while the darker ring represents the winter months when little or no growth occurred. The two together make up one complete year's growth. Depending on the year, growth can be rapid (thick summer growth rings) or slow. Each year makes its own unique pattern.

Stratigraphy

Stratigraphy, which means the study and comparison of separate layers of deposits that build up over time, is another relative dating method. This method helps archaeologists establish the order in which objects were made or used. Tells, like the one shown below, provide a good example of how stratigraphy works.

Some sites have been inhabited for thousands of years. Layer upon layer of debris build up, with the most recent houses on top and the oldest on the bottom. As archaeologists dig, they uncover the various levels, or strata, and are able to date the artifacts within them as older or more recent than those above or below.

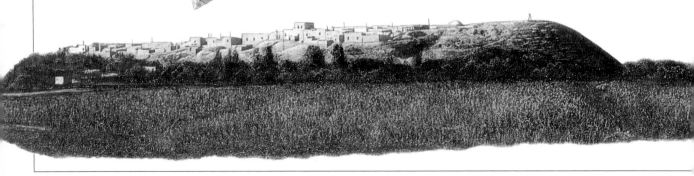

Radiocarbon dating

Radiocarbon, or Carbon 14 (written C-14), is one of the most useful dating methods because it can be used to date anything that has ever been alive (wood, bones, plants, animals, etc.). C-14 is a radioactive element produced by the atmosphere and absorbed by plants. It is passed on to animals, including humans, in the food chain. When a living thing dies the C-14 begins to decay. Scientists know the rate at which it decays, so by measuring the amount of C-14 left in an object they can tell how long ago it died. It can be used to date objects up to around 40,000 years old.

Thermoluminescence

Thermoluminescence, known as TL dating, is used to date pottery. All pottery contains radioactive elements that build up at a known rate over time. When a pot is heated, all the TL is released and the radioactive count returns to zero. Scientists know that the pot was fired when it was made. When they reheat it the TL that has accumulated in the meantime is measured and an exact date of manufacture can be established. TL dating is also used to date burnt flints. It is effective on items up to around 80,000 years old.

Since pottery is the most common item found on archaeological sites from Neolithic times onward, TL dating is very useful.

Potassium-argon dating is especially useful when it comes to dating the oldest human remains, like this Australopithecus boisei *skull, which dates to around 1.8 million years ago.*

Potassium-argon dating

Like C-14 and TL dating, the potassium-argon method is based on the known rate of decay of a radioactive element. In this case it measures the decay at which potassium decays into argon gas in volcanic rocks. Since the rate of decay is very slow, this method is suitable for dating rocks that are over 100,000 years old.

Early calendars

Calendars used by ancient people can be useful dating tools. When archaeologists have identified one or two known events in an ancient calendar, they can use these to read and date other events recorded on the calendar.

The Aztec Calendar Stone has the symbols of the 20-day Aztec calendar running around the edge of the disc.

Historical records and the end of prehistory

Prehistory is said to end and history begin from the time when people started to keep written records. Writing was first invented in Mesopotamia and Egypt around 5,300 years ago. Various forms of writing were invented in many different regions over the following centuries. A few groups, such as the Australian Aborigines, never had a written language.

Examples of some early forms of writing: 1. Mesopotamian cuneiform clay tablet; 2. early Chinese pictographs; 3. Maya codex; 4. seal with writing from Mohenjo-Daro in ancient India; 5. Egyptian hieroglyph.

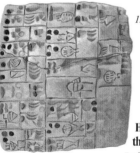

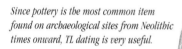

1.

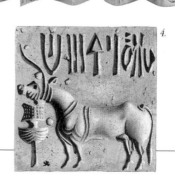

3.

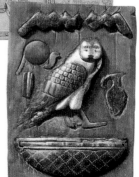
5.

4.

2.

Glossary

diet The food that an organism consumes to survive.

domesticate To tame an animal. Human beings have been domesticating certain animals, such as dogs and horses, for thousands of years.

hearth A hearth is an area in a home or other dwelling where fires are built, such as a fireplace.

hunter-gatherer Hunter-gatherers were people who survived by foraging for plants and hunting animals. Hunter-gatherers had a mobile existence, and seldom settled in one place for very long.

irrigation The practice of supplying land used for farming or other agricultural purposes with water.

kiln An oven that is generally used to fire clay pottery.

linen A woven textile that is made from plant fibers.

livestock Animals that are raised for agricultural purposes.

megalith A large monument made out of stone that is generally believed to have had a religious or spiritual function.

mortar and pestle This tool, made from two components, is used to grind various substances. The pestle is a sticklike object with a rounded end that is used to grind or pulverize materials in the mortar, which is a bowl.

ochre A kind of earth.

perishable Something that can decompose.

prehistory A period of time that existed before written human history.

primate A biological order of mammals that includes modern humans.

sickle A tool with a curved blade that is used to cut grass, hay and crops.

terracotta A kind of clay pottery that is fired in a kiln, but is not glazed.

For More Information

Canadian Museum of Civilization
100 Laurier Street
Gatineau, QC K1A 0M8
Canada
(819) 776-7000
Web site: http://www.civilization.ca/cmc/home/cmc-home
This museum has showcases on the history of human beings in Canada and houses exhibits of prehistoric artifacts.

Metropolitan Museum of Art
1000 Fifth Avenue
New York, NY 10028-0198
(212) 535-7710
Web site: http://www.metmuseum.org
The Metropolitan Museum of Art is home to a wide-ranging collection of art, artifacts and exhibits.

National Geographic Society
1145 17th Street NW
Washington, DC 20036-4688
(800) 647 5463
Web site: http://events.nationalgeographic.com
Founded in 1888, the National Geographic Society is a nonprofit organization dedicated to archaeology, geography and natural science.

National Museum of Natural History
P.O. Box 37012
Smithsonian Institute
Washington DC 20013-7012
Web site: http://www.mnh.si.edu
The National Museum of Natural History contains a wealth of artifacts from ancient and prehistoric peoples.

Web Sites
Due to the changing nature of Internet links, Rosen Publishing has developed an online list of Web sites related to the subject of this book. This site is updated regularly. Please use this link to access the list:

http://www.rosenlinks.com/aac/preh

For Further Reading

Aczel, Amir D. *The Cave and the Cathedral: How a Real-Life Indiana Jones and a Renegade Scholar Decoded the Ancient Art of Man*. Hoboken, NJ: John Wiley & Sons, Inc., 2009.

Aujoulat, Norbert. *Lascaux: Movement, Space, and Time*. New York, NY: Harry N. Abrams, 2005.

Bahn, Paul. *Cave Art: A Guide to the Decorated Ice Age Caves of Europe*. London, UK: Frances Lincoln Ltd., 2007.

Clottes, Jean. *Cave Art*. London: Phaidon Press, Inc., 2008.

Clottes, Jean. *Chauvet Cave: The Art of Earliest Times*. Salt Lake City, UT: University of Utah Press, 2003.

Cunliffe, Barry, ed. *The Oxford Illustrated History of Prehistoric Europe*. New York, NY: Oxford University Press, 2001.

Curtis, Gregory. *The Cave Painters: Probing the Mysteries of the World's First Artists*. New York, NY: Anchor Books, 2006.

Hodder, Ian. *The Leopard's Tale: Revealing the Mysteries of Çatalhöyük*. New York, NY: Thames & Hudson, 2006.

Jones, Carleton. *Temples of Stone: Exploring the Megalithic Tombs of Ireland*. Doughcloyne, Wilton, Cork, Ireland: Collins Press, 2007.

Malone, Carline, Nancy Stone Bernard, and Brian Fagan. *Stonehenge*. New York, NY: Oxford University Press, 2002.

Morris, Neil. *Everyday Life in Prehistory*. Florence, Italy: McRae Books, 2005.

Roberts, J.M. *Prehistory and the First Civilizations*. New York, NY: Oxford University Press, 2002.

White, Randall. *Prehistoric Art: The Symbolic Journey of Humankind*. New York: Harry N. Abrams, 2003.

Whitley, David S. *Cave Paintings and the Human Spirit: The Origin of Creativity and Belief*. Amherst, NY: Prometheus Books, 2009.

Index

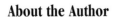

About the Author

Beatrice D. Brooke is a writer from upstate New York.

The publishers would like to thank the following picture libraries and photographers for permission to reproduce their photos:

Cover (right, top to bottom): Cover (right, top to bottom): © www.istockphoto.com/David Rock, © www.istockphoto.com/ Javier Garcîa Blanco, © www.istockphoto.com/Tim Messick, © www.istockphoto.com/Juergen Bosse

16–17 Scala Group, Florence; 29 A. Woolfitt/Corbis; 30–31 Ministère Français de la Culture et de la Communication, DRAC Rhône-Alpes, Service Régional de l'Archéologie.